The New Civil War

Michael A. Banks, PhD

Dedicated to the memory of Tamir Rice, Jordan Davis and the children of Sandy Hook Elementary School.

The New Civil War
Copyright © 2018 Michael A. Banks, PhD

Library of Congress Control Number:	2019935297
Paperback:	978-1-950024-24-7
eBook:	978-1-950024-26-1
Hardcover:	978-1-950024-25-4

BOOK-ART
PRESS SOLUTIONS

30 Wall Street, 8th Floor
New York City, NY 10005
www.bookartpress.us
+1-800-351-3529

CONTENTS

FOREWORD

This is a study that will concentrate on the invisible time frame within the step-by-step accounts of an encounter leading to the infamous and ultimate death of a black youth in America. It is by no means an accurate or professional diagnosis of the incident, and also does not directly blame any one individual or institution as to the outcome of the verdict or make any direct inferences that the study may tend to insinuate. From the outset of this study, it was never intended as an attempt to re-try the case, but an attempt to invoke speculation in order to understand misconception. It does not intend to imply anything specific, and could be wrong about everything that it may insinuate, however most of the material asks questions that are designed to make the reader think and contemplate answers as to the incident itself and the verdict as well; so as to create theories as to what can be done in the future toward the prevention of further such incidents. The answer to any of the questions that are spread throughout this text is either yes, no or rhetorical.

Despite their often flawed reports, society generally tends to "believe" the media in substance; accepts certain opinions and adopts certain opinions on events. The media serves the function as one of the foremost keepers and propagators of social values, and serves as a great influence in the shaping of public opinion; as many landmark cases are tried in the media before the case itself gets to court, or even before an arrest and/ or arraignment is made (i.e. Lee Harvey Oswald, O. J. Simpson, Jerry Sandusky, etc.) As media is highly instrumental in the formation of social opinions, the groundwork of this effort will be a study based on electronic media, articles, facts of the case, a nationally televised trial and subsequent acquittal of the defendant; including new developments that have taken place in the aftermath of the verdict. As the incident and verdict were heavily and thoroughly mediated, the study will entertain several popular media-enhanced adversarial viewpoints and opinions.

Apart from social inequality, racism, gun control, gun laws and other controversies which are equally important issues, the focal objective of this study is more concerned about the safety of our children and the advancement of society in terms of social policy and social equality. It is a look at the incident and the verdict through various theoretical perspectives of sociology as a guideline; the emergence of the incident and the outcome of the verdict are far reaching in the social imagination and involve many unasked and unanswered questions. This tragic incident involving the two parties entails many bigger pictures and suggests that there is a war going on right here in our society. The new civil war hypothesizes a current war between grown adults and children, as the blood of children (including many infants) is beginning to drench the soil and streets of America, and many of these children are the young victims of firearms. Whether this young man was killed due to reasons of self-defense, racism, psychosis and/ or malicious impulsivity, one thing is painfully certain: another child is dead.

This will be an effort to mobilize the citizens of society, in an effort to look at the incident in the same manner as we look at reality, as we all presumably love our children. Personal opinions need to be shelved in place of group goals in an effort to retain the objective dignity of the American community in the areas of "life, liberty and the pursuit of happiness". Many members of certain social groups' interpretation and beliefs of those words do not feel guaranteed by the lettering of the implied rights, while others may feel over-privileged in its interpretation and believability; and this has historically shown its evidence in the American courtroom. It is the duty of the great American society to come to an agreed conclusion of this tragic incident, before it may have to agree on something even more significant. The future safety of our children should be a priority that we concern ourselves with, because this is a war that they are losing. It is also a civil war of many opposing new ideas and arguments in the areas of child safety, gun control, and racism among others. Even if the defendant was convicted, there is nothing any of us can do to bring back the plaintiff, but there is the possibility of saving future potential endangered children simply with an adjustment in laws, and an adjustment of the attitudes of social members, in terms of mutual respect for one another. It is something we should have rap sessions, meeting, conferences, and lengthy symposiums about because prevention is probably the most important ingredient to the cure. It is something we can do as a society and it is the duty of our democracy to address any social problem, and this is where we begin; again.

INTRODUCTION

Sociologists basically use theoretical perspectives to explain the emergence of society. These perspectives act as a framework for understanding social phenomenon such as racism, social deviance, criminology and social pathology. In an approach to this highly-publicized incident, this study will utilize three perspectives of sociological theory: (1) conflict theory (2) structural-functionalism (3) symbolic interaction.

Radical or *Conflict* theory among the other various perspectives of sociology is an oft-used measure in an approach to formulate a thesis, book, article or term paper. According to noted theorists such as C. Wright Mills and Karl Marx, the conflict theory of society implies that social structure has emerged through competition and conflict, as society is fragmented into groups that compete for social and economic resources. It is a theory that also explains the social functions of crime and racism in terms as by-products of a capitalistic system; and a theory that explores alternate systems that might generate more harmonious social relations. Radical criminology suggests that society is ever-changing; that crime is caused by the social and economic forces of society and is in the interests of the ruling class, or power elite. Power is defined by those with the greatest political, economic and social resources, and that power and coercion produce social order; order that is maintained by domination. This theory tends to view criminal behavior as an instrument by which the powerful and affluent coerce the poor into patterns of behavior that preserve the status quo. Conflict theorists insist that deviant behaviors are actions that do not comply with, and are a threat, to and across social institutions. However, in an attempt to analyze this case, incident and ultimate verdict from the trial, this study does not pretend to be objective, because of the fact that a child was killed by an adult in a situation that could have been totally avoided; and through a motive which could have been racial, impulsive, as well as psychotic. This study does not view self-defense as an option because the defendant was already defending himself before he began his pursuit of the plaintiff; before he left his automobile; before he became the aggressor. By leaving his vehicle to pursue the plaintiff on foot, and against the strongly suggested advice of his superiors, indicates the point at which he forfeited that right. Social conflict among the American masses has resulted, as a product of the nature of this homicidal incident and the eventual verdict from the trial. Many view the homicide as a crime, while many others, including the jury, interpreted the defendant's actions as self-defense and in the interests of the ruling class. As a case in point, this study also addresses questions surrounding the *role* of the State Attorney's Office in that state in (1) the gathering of critical information by the local police department (2) their presentation of the evidence and (3) the resulting not guilty verdict.

As formulated by noted social theorist Emile D̃ ̇ev̇

"father of sociology"), *structural-functional* theory suggests

self-regulating and racial incidents such as this one, as well

lead to social change. The main argument of this theory is ᴛʜᴀᴛ ᴏᴄᴄᴇᴇ,

composed of individuals, groups, organizations and institutions, and thriving

on consensus and cooperation. The social system is hypothetically and

analogously compared to the various input and output systems of the human

body; as a means to a whole. In cases of crime, civil/ social unrest and/ or

social upheaval, or any factors that would upset social stability, the society

will always return to a state of homeostasis, or a return to order. According

to this theory, crime is "functional" for the self-regulation of society, in that

individuals learn the boundaries of accepted human behavior through the

punishment of criminals. The totality of beliefs and sentiments make up the

"collective conscience" (or "the glue of society") and forms *the moral basis* that

is common to all members of society; as the collective conscience is said to

be produced through social interaction. Structural-functionalism theory as it

applies to the over-demonstrative impact of the verdict, with respect to the

angry millions of individuals nationwide, represents "disequilibrium" in the

social system in response to the incident and the verdict. This abnormality in

the social system is highly reflective of the idea that a well-publicized killer

was not punished. The masses who were heavily in favor of and supported a

defendant victory are also part of this disequilibrium process; as the society

has not returned to normal because of this major issue (and other related

issues), and has caused objectivity in this study to be somewhat difficult to

maintain. The defendant was found not guilty through a preponderance of dence/ character witnesses and cleared through a jury of his peers, despite evidence to the contrary and evidence that was never introduced. Discussions about race were withheld from the trial and the defendant's criminal history was never in question, as the verdict is still discussed and debated in a national forum. Gun control and the Second Amendment will also be addressed. As a case in point, this study wants to discuss the rationale of the gun industry as well as the sanity of gun owners.

Symbolic-interactionist perspective suggests that society was created, connected through and thrives on social interaction. "People act toward things based on the meaning that these things have for them" (Blumer, 1986). This theory attempts to explain how people use symbols to create meaning; meanings that are derived through social interaction and modified through interpretation. Instantly, this theory suggests that the defendant profiled the deceased plaintiff in reaction to his skin color, his actions, and the way he was dressed, through the defendant's own learned value system. He allegedly perceived the plaintiff to be a threat to himself and the symbol of a black menace, and he relayed that inflamed information to a police non-emergency dispatch operator before he took the plaintiff's life. By the standard legal mandates of due process of law, normal police procedures were uncustomarily broken as evidenced by his original non-arrest, and appears in effect to have led to further perceived legal "*misprocedures*" in this case. With respect to society and the masses who did not agree with the verdict, both the incident and the verdict symbolize and reflect historical injustice, social inequality and bias within the legal system. When convictions and acquittals of this magnitude are unjustly served, bad precedents are set, both in the law and the society at hand.

This study will look at the incident and the verdict through these different perspectives, however there is also a revisionist element to this case. It appears that radical and racial events in American social history tend to repeat many times over before change becomes apparent. As a parallel, the racial incidents and verdicts of Emmett Till, Rodney King and OJ Simpson will be used in analogy or a comparison to this case, because these events are in symbolic contrast to each other in the social imagination. As noted historically, similar incidents and events will re-occur even after there is change, making the society strive for social goals that have already been achieved, and in this manner the advancement of the coexistence of the races in America remains stifled; society "never gets anywhere"; in the manner of "two steps forward and one step back".

PROLOGUE

The not guilty verdict for the defendant didn't just fill the masses with outrage and anger; it also filled them with curiosity and questions. The Government wants them to accept the verdict and praise the US legal system for being the best in the world. Should they also accept the verdict that allowed the murderers of Emmett Till to walk free; the murderers who bragged in an exclusive interview a month later to a national magazine *(Look Magazine)* about how and why they lynched the 14-year old? Should they accept the legal decision that exonerated the murderers who blew up a church and ultimately killed four Sunday school children in Alabama in 1963; and the decision of the Justice Department to withhold evidence from the case? Should they accept the decision to acquit the four (?) policemen involved in the Rodney King beating, when those officers ruthlessly and repeatedly struck him with lead-filled batons (all of which was caught on video/ displayed on national television) and later claimed that he was resisting arrest? In addition, should they also accept the countless decisions from the many other historically atrocious legal verdicts that promote the image and symbol of white supremacy as well? It is unlikely that the masses will ever accept this decision. The verdict just doesn't sit well with them. Millions, including both Americans and foreigners of all nationalities, were not satisfied by many of the explanations that pointed to his apparent manufactured innocence. This study will be addressing many of the skepticisms that have arisen; and unasked questions involving this case.

In times of social change, there are many recurring themes that play out before that change is met. In this case, a 16-year old teenager was returning home in the rain from the local store carrying a drink and a bag of candy, and was ultimately shot and killed in a gated community by an off-duty neighborhood watchman. The killer assumed that the teenager was a suspicious character. As such, he followed him with a 9mm semi-automatic pistol, shot and killed the teenager following almost a minute of monumental screaming and pleading. The gunman was taken into custody, no charges were filed, and he was set free after a brief interrogation by the police. The teenager was taken to the morgue and classified as a John Doe; was identified two days later and American public outcry led by major civil rights' activists demanded the killer's arrest.

Under heavy public and media pressure, the newly-appointed State Prosecutor arranged for the killer to be brought to justice. The mother of the neighborhood watchman exclaimed that her son was brought in (arrested) to calm down the crowds. He was re-arrested by the police six weeks later and charged with murder in the first degree. The original mishandling of the forensics by the department, as well as the not filing of any charges, no criminal background check, no drug test, the release of a homicide suspect and the re-issuing of his gun, raises questions to the reasonably intelligent.

Also very unusual, why did the medical examiner have no recollection of an autopsy procedure that he performed on such a major figure of a landmark and over-mediated case, only a little over a year after the incident? Many basic themes did not come into question during the murder trial, and some were disallowed from the trial altogether. Also, the defendant was not required to testify on the witness stand as to his homicidal actions. Was the "not guilty" verdict the product of an organized collection of interests?

After a strenuous 3-week nationally televised murder in front of a 6-woman jury (5 white, one Hispanic of mixed race), the defendant was acquitted of all charges. The impact of this homicide and verdict has disrupted the very fabric of the American nation, causing racial tension and controversy in the society. Not since the ultimate exoneration of the killers of Emmett Till in 1955, and to an extent the impact of the Rodney King beating, along with the OJ Simpson trial, had a media-enhanced racial incident and ultimate legal verdict captured and divided the opinions of Americans up to that point. At the same time, the defendant had a tremendous following and many supporters who carried racial agendas. People of all shades and nationalities are marching for justice where perceived injustice was served, in an attempt to create social change and a revision of laws.

There are many coincidental/ recurring themes here. Favorable decisions for the perpetrators of hate crimes is the first. The name "King", as in Martin Luther King and Rodney King; as history tends to repeat itself. Another recurrence is the fact that both the victim and Emmett Till bought candy before they died. It's hard to believe that candy would lead to a kid's demise. Yet it has.

FACTS OF THE CASE

1. The victim and a younger friend were both together playing video games and watching the NBA All-Star Game on television one night at a residence in the gated community. The victim left the house at the beginning of halftime to buy snacks for himself and the friend.

2. On the way back from the store, the victim was spotted by the watchman who instantly called a non-emergency dispatch (311) to report the number of break-ins at the complex (relative to the "suspicious" character that he was observing).

3. He identified the suspicious character as looking black, wearing a hoodie, and looking like he's up to no good, like he's on drugs or something, staring...

4. The watchman reported that the subject was looking at him, that he had his hand in his waistband, that he didn't know what his deal was. Suddenly he exclaimed that the suspect had something in his hand, as if he is being threatened by the character. Dispatch operator says, just let me know if this guy does anything else. Watchman replies, ok; these assholes, they always get away, which implies that his suspect must now be moving away from him and no longer a threat.

5. This 311 call continued for approximately another 60 seconds of back and forth conversation with the dispatch about what entrance the police should use when they arrive, and even though the suspect didn't appear to be a threat at this time, the watchman suddenly replies that the suspect is running.

6. Under his normal voice tone, he made the remark, fucking coons! Still on the 311, the operator could hear a gush of wind and heavy breath in the telephone line and asked the watchman if he was following him. The watchman replied affirmative.

7. The 311 operator *then suggested that the watchman not follow the subject*. Watchman replied, ok.

8. While still on the line, the listener can still hear the wind in the microphone, as if the other party was still in pursuit (running) and breathing hard. Suddenly the watchman identified himself and relayed the fact that the subject ran away.

9. The watchman then described his location to the operator, making arrangements as to where he police can meet him at the complex.

10. The watchman then changed the plan, telling the operator instead the number that *he* can be reached at, while still following the subject. This is the point at which the watchman appeared to have again caught sight of the suspect, and also the point at which he lost communication with the dispatch officer.

11. [Invisible time frame begins] Through these deliberate steps, the watchman finally confronted the suspect and asked him what he

was doing there, according to an ear witness, Madame K, who was on the phone with the suspect when he was accosted. She originally heard him tell the watchman to get off of him, and this was followed by a resounding shove and a cellphone that had fallen into the grass.

12. An altercation ensued, at least 45 seconds of resounding screams and cries for help, a gunshot, and then silence, all of which were picked up through the few 911 calls that neighbors made to the police. [Invisible time frame ends]

13. Police officials arrived and found the suspect dead with his arms underneath him and a bullet hole through his heart and lung.

14. The watchman was found by police with slight lacerations, a disfigured nose and bruises to his head.

15. The watchman was taken into custody, questioned for approximately 2 hours and released.

16. The teenage suspect was taken to the morgue and not identified for two days.

17. Under heavy media and public pressure, the State Prosecutor re-arrested the watchman six weeks later, and charged him with murder in the first degree.

18. The watchman was ultimately acquitted by a 6-woman (5 white, one Hispanic) jury and cleared of all charges 2 years later.

Fact 3 is the watchman's original typecast of the suspect (i.e. wearing a hoodie, he appears to "look" black, and also looks like he's up to no good).

Fact 4 is the watchman's presumed threat by the subject (i.e. he's coming towards me…he's got something in his waistband, I don't know what his deal is). It is here that he is warning the 311 dispatch that he may be in fear of his life, basing that notion on the presence of the appearance of the suspect advancing toward his car. Fact 5 gives the assumption that the suspect is no longer a "threat", as he appears to be moving away from the watchman, who stated to the dispatch, these assholes always get away. As the threat appeared to have subsided at this point, exactly one minute later he suddenly and clearly exclaims that the suspect is running. Question, what offensive or criminal act did the suspect commit prior to or after he began running? Is running itself a crime? Could he have run because a man was stalking him in a car? It is at this point that the watchman presumably leaves his automobile to begin his armed pursuit of the suspect, as noted by the automobile door chimes that signaled the opening of his door and the rush of the wind in the microphone of the 311 call. The watchman states, "fucking coons" and this is followed by, "are you following him?", 1.0 seconds later by the 311 dispatch operator. The watchman replied affirmative and the operator suggested that he not take that action. The watchman instantly ignored the suggestion not to follow and continued to pursue the suspect. Fact 10-11 implies that while the watchman was still in pursuit, the dispatch asks him his name, to which he replied his name, and offered the information that the suspect ran, suggesting that the suspect must have disappeared from his sight at that point. This is the point that the watchman and the operator try to corroborate and make arrangements as to what entrance the police should use when they arrive. Fact 12 indicates the point that the watchman apparently regained sight of the suspect and tells the dispatch the phone number that *he* can be reached and ultimately ended the conversation. Facts 13 and 14 suggest the "invisible time frame" and the period in which the watchman apprehended, shot and killed the suspect. The 911 calls to the police by neighbors have picked up the only transmissions of the screaming and pleading that was heard during the altercation, and the last 45-50 seconds of his life; one neighbor who was terrified during the call said the screams sounded like a young boy. Madame K was also on the phone with the suspect at the beginning of the altercation, however the reproduction of that call was never brought in as an exhibit to the Court and her general testimony was ruled as not credible.

The neighborhood watch at the gated community is a voluntary position that the watchman himself initiated, in accordance with the neighborhood watch program as supervised by the local police. He began this program almost two years after he bought the pistol that ended the suspect's life, and only five months before he shot and killed the suspect. The neighborhood watch supervisor testified that the watchman contacted and came to her to get the program started. Throughout the whole confrontation, the watchman never identified himself as a watchman to the suspect, nor was he dressed or gave any physical impression that he was a security guard. It's possible that the teenager was afraid of his appearance. It is also doubtful that the tenant who the suspect was visiting even knew the watchman, or even knew of his position. How many tenants actually knew him, or knew of him prior to this incident?

Another question or speculation could be, by the fact that the suspect had already been staying at the complex for a few days before the incident, did the watchman recognize the suspect at the complex maybe days before the incident, or a day before, deem his character and appearance "suspicious" according to his learned value system, have an ongoing vendetta against him, but did not know he was visiting a tenant? Every adjective that he used to describe the suspect was that of a bad and suspicious character, in his assumption that the suspect fit the description of the perpetrators of break-ins at his gated community. Could he have made more of an effort to find out if the suspect was a visitor, or a resident for that matter? Did the watchman know that the suspect was a visitor and the two had a prior altercation, and this time the watchman made sure to bring his pistol to work? In the opinion of this study, the prosecution missed a lot. They should have questioned all aspects of premeditation and all (or at least a sample) of the tenants to find out how many of them were familiar with the neighborhood watchman, either personally, impersonally, or not at all. The watchman should have been required to take the witness stand as well.

EMMETT TILL AND THE SUSPECT – A PARALLEL

E mmett Till was a 14-year old black male from Chicago, Illinois. Prior to the vacation trip to his uncle's house in Money, Mississippi, he was warned by his mother to behave in such a manner so as not to disturb the racist fabric of the South in 1955. Given to his Northern ways, Till made the mistake of "wolf-whistling" at a Caucasian woman in a grocery store in the Mississippi neighborhood, while buying some gum. The woman, Carol Bryant, reacted spontaneously to her perceived indiscretion of Till's gesture. She went out to her car to get a pistol, as Till, his uncle and cousins scurried off in the uncle's car. Later that week, two white men with guns drawn, Roy Bryant (husband of Carolyn) and JW Milam (brother of Roy) arrived at the uncle's house, dragged Till out of his bed and into a waiting vehicle, explaining to the uncle that they just wanted to "talk to the boy". Till was kidnapped from the house, tortured and murdered. He was beat in the head with pistols, his 14-year old face appeared to be burned off with acid, his eyes were gouged and removed, chopped across the nose with an axe and shot through the head. The body was disposed of in the nearby Tallahatchie River.

After the undertaker reluctantly opened the coffin in Chicago, Till's mother stated that she could see right through the bullet hole in Emmett's head clear to the other side, and that one of his eyes was lying on his chest. For the record, after one hour of deliberation, the two killers were acquitted of charges of kidnapping and murder before an all-white male jury in Mississippi, who reasoned that the corpse was so water-logged and disfigured that it was unrecognizable and could not be identified. The body that was removed from the river, however, still had his late father's (Louis Till) ring on a finger; a ring that bore the initials "LT", and a ring that was given to him by his mother prior to the trip. Some of the jury were convinced of the guilt of the named perpetrators, however they didn't feel like the killing of a black person was worth two white men going to jail for the rest of their lives. The accumulative punishment to Till was beyond macabre, beyond savage. An accurate word to describe the Till lynching would be "monstrous". His mutilated body was discovered at the bottom of a river, and his neck was bound to a cotton gin by barbed wire. Emmett Till was killed in a demonstration of pure and vicious racial hatred.

The story of this lynching and photographs of the body throughout the national media outraged the growing black American masses of the 1950's, and inspired numerous black protests throughout the nation, including the famous one-woman "Rosa Parks Movement" just two months later. The use of the cotton gin to help submerge Till's body into a river was most likely done through symbolic intent by these murderers, because the machine itself was invented by a black slave to lessen and ease the work of other black who worked the cotton fields (as Eli Whitney is wrongfully given the credit for this invention, but nonetheless patented it in 1794). Southern rumors went so far as to suggest that the NAACP "planted" the body so as to upset the status quo of the Jim Crow South in an effort to promote their brand. The murderers probably got increased satisfaction from the killing of a black child for the perceived indiscretion through the use of this symbolism, while simultaneously denouncing the black invention (as this type of racism relates cotton to black people); for the purpose of sending a symbolic deterrent message of murderous hatred to all other blacks, as stated by the murderers. Despite the many achievements of blacks in the arts and sciences up to that point in time (1955), and including the collective patriotism of the black troops that emanated from the recent victorious World War II and Korean War efforts, "Jim Crow" legislation ("separate but equal" laws that were adopted coincidentally with the end of slavery and the Civil War, in an effort to keep blacks oppressed as a social group) was still fully enforced in the United States, and white racism toward blacks was as outrageous/ ridiculous as ever. The Reverend Dr. Martin Luther King (Southern Christian Leadership Conference) would emerge as the foremost spokesman in America on the matter of civil rights, justice and equality in America, as a result of the Rosa Parks stand, and he also adopted her method of "passive resistance" in his future endeavors.

The social significance of most civil rights issues that come to the forefront of American politics usually begins with tragedies such as Emmett Till and the teenaged suspect. It has to do with the audacity of the determine that a life is expendable and less than equal to their

ıtchman case reflected a "wannabe-a-cop" attitude description

lant, and a "wannabe" type of cop that has historically been given exoneration for the shooting and killing of innocent black adults and children. As a direct result of his apparent growing psychoses, which probably coincides with the duration of his having a gun permit and owning a gun, he wanted to be recognized and respected by the general public as a cop or someone in authority who had something to do with law enforcement, in delusional terms, even without having to produce the necessary identification or display a recognizable uniform. The watchman previously expressed an interest in law enforcement to the administrative manager of the police department, and once stated how high a regard he has for law officers. The manager testified as to the watchman's ambition to do ride-alongs with real policemen, in order to solidify his chances at one day becoming a police officer. It makes one wonder about the mental stability of some of the officers that are currently in uniform, including military. How many police officers began with the same mindset as the watchman?

The watchman had a unique problem, not uncommon among wannabes of this nature, a racial identity problem. He is part Caucasian and Mestizo. His outward personality is what they would call "Uncle Tom" (a historical device used by ethnic and racial groups as a form of assimilation, acculturation and conformity to the American white race). This device is usually expressed in the physical display of mannerisms, speech, views, alteration of physical characteristics such as hair or skin color, and other characteristics of the majority group that have been adopted and incorporated into the behavior and appearance of the individual. The individual adopts this behavior and mannerisms with the objective of receiving the approval, fair and/ or special treatment by members of the majority society, as opposed to what he/ she perceives as the general and ethical mistreatment by the majority toward his or some other minority/ ethnic groups; and for the purpose of being accepted as "white" by the general society. Apparently, when he is pretending to be a cop on the neighborhood watch job, he is presumably *acting and thinking as a racially-profiling white cop,* or how he believes that racist white cop would act and think like. This particular homicide of a black teenager appeared to be a stereotypical imitation of white cops who have actually been acquitted for the killing of innocent black people (Amadou Diallo, Sean Bell, etc.) in American society, and to a great extent the not guilty verdict reflects most of the other atrocious legal verdicts that have been passed down throughout the history of race in America, including the initial legal exoneration of the LA cops who were recorded and later displayed on national television inflicting police brutality on the person of Rodney King.

This particular homicide was against a kid who had dreams and ambitions of rocket science, of going to the moon, but that dream is lost because of a situation that could have been totally avoided. The watchman's apparent racial act is obviously an insult to good cops. In the opinion of this study, this act together with the theme of racism has shamed the whole country in front of the world, and the acquittal was a slap in the face to Americans, according to one prominent figure. The arresting officer described the subject as a good kid with a good family, not a goon. He explained to the watchman that he didn't just kill some black delinquent, miscreant and/ or deviant kid that no one cared about; not that it should matter. The officer seemed to understand that the death of this black child appeared to be attached with a note of disregard for human life. He stated that this was a kid with a future, a kid with folks who care, and that he basically made a victim out of the wrong person. The watchman, however, was set free. The police did not conduct a toxicology report or a criminal background check on the watchman, as was done immediately to the suspect. As well, critical forensic evidence was mishandled and/ or lost, especially in the area of the transference of blood and other DNA.

Years before, the watchman actually took a course at a criminal justice college that thoroughly covered all the self-defense laws of that state, meaning that *he studied and perfected the preconceived notion of having to file such a claim.* In layman's terms, he basically may have wanted to kill somebody and get away with it by claiming self-defense; or maybe he specifically wanted to kill a black person as a trophy. A retired defense lawyer stated that it was possible that he could create a narrative about the incident, but the forensics would be more difficult to match up. The watchman received an "A" for the course, as his professor testified that he was one of the best students in his class. For the record, the watchman was placed on academic probation from the college due to underachievement in his other courses, and in danger of termination from the institution. If this was his academic situation, the question becomes, *why did he express diligence and excel in that particular course?*

WAS THIS A HATE CRIME? – WHY WAS 'RACE' DISALLOWED FROM THE CASE?

From the outset, the Court did not allow the theme of race to enter or dominate the case. The judge also did not allow the term "racial profiling" to be mentioned in the courtroom. Although both sides agreed that the case was not about race, could it be that race was the key factor and motivation in the death of the suspect, and the correct avenue for coming to a conclusion to the real truth of the matter? This case had everything to do with race. A reporter from a national newspaper wrote that the watchman would warn the residents at the complex to be careful of young black males, and that he appeared to be fixated on black males. His ex-fiancé had recently testified in a case against the watchman that his whole family was racist, and didn't like her because she wasn't white; wanted him to marry a white girl. He was charged with rape, battery and molestation in that case. He was also charged in another case of the repeated child molestation of a relative (niece) who can attest to his racism and his confrontational behavior.

Identity concealed, she testified that the watchman's family didn't like black people if they didn't *act* like white people; that they like black people if they act white. Testimony from those cases were not allowed in the trial, however, because it was felt that it would bias the jury. Toxicology reports of the suspect's post-mortem positive drug test for marijuana use were used in the defense's closing statements, however; although he had no criminal record. The watchman did have run-ins with the law and once fought with a policeman, but was not given a drug test after killing the suspect. Was this a fair trial?

The watchman's foot pursuit of the suspect began with the words, "fucking coons". These are the words that one can hear prior to the question, are you following him? (during the non-emergency 311 call that he made to police while in pursuit of a 16-year old). These assholes always get away, stated an angry and frustrated watchman to the dispatch one minute before the pursuit. From his numerous routine petty complaints and over-descriptions of suspicious-looking black characters at the housing complex to his apparent setting up 311 for an actual shooting of a human being, we have witnessed a person gone steadily out of control, and was over-zealous in his approach to the voluntary job. It is already known of his numerous calls to 911 reporting the suspicious nature of black characters who, in his opinion, didn't look like they belonged at or near the gated community. At one point in the communication with the dispatch, he again reminded the operator that the suspect was a black male without being asked. The watchman proceeded that the suspect looked like he was up to no good, like he's on drugs, and that he was progressively becoming a threat as the suspect, while walking on the sidewalk, was approaching the watchman's car. As the suspect passed his car and was walking to his destination, the watchman exclaimed to the operator that this asshole was getting away, one minute before the pursuit. After a minute, he sees the suspect running, when he exclaims that fact to the operator. In the opinion of this study, the watchman would have had to make a u-turn to notice that the suspect was running or which direction he ran. He had already walked past the watchman's car. Once past, the suspect would have been walking away from the watchman's back. With all of his statements to the dispatch, he was apparently setting up 311 for the alleged belief that he personally felt threatened by this person and knowing that he has a loaded pistol in his possession, he is apparently contemplating whether to shoot and kill him. I don't know what his deal is, apparently expresses a direct personal threat in the watchman's perception and he may have already premeditated the ultimate confrontation and the alibi at this point. It appears as though he is already claiming self-defense with these pre-homicide statements to the dispatch. If the suspect was perceived by the watchman to be such a menace, why didn't he call the emergency number (911) as opposed to the non-emergency number? Was he told not to call 911 anymore with his constant calls? Is it because he knew the suspect was not committing a crime and not actually a threat? When he reported that the suspect was running, that should have been the end of his so-called assumed/ perceived threat and the end of his duty for that particular case as a neighborhood watchman; and after finishing his dialogue with the dispatch, he should have never left his car at that point and/or should have just let the police take over the situation, which would have been a pure act of self-preservation, but no. The *"running" is what signaled the watchman to action,* and his physically armed pursuit of the suspect. Question: Could it be that the subject started to run because he was slowly being followed by a man in an automobile?

Instead of letting the profiled perpetrator "run", as he stated to 311, and instead of letting the cops go after the perpetrator, and as his neighborhood watch superiors testified in Court that the neighborhood watch program was not designed to be vigilant, and after having been advised what would be the right course of action, he disobeys the order and pursues.

The head of the National Sheriff's Association explained *emphasized* that the neighborhood watch do not possess police powers, carry weapons or pursue vehicles; *to report as opposed to pursue.* The watchman's superiors made it clear that you are never to pursue a suspect. On that night, the confrontational spirit of the watchman defied all of the rules that guide a neighborhood watchman, and instructed him to make the decision to perform the role as vigilante and take the law into his own hands. This was one individual that the watchman made it a purpose that he was not going to let get away. He then pursued the profiled black perpetrator with a bullet already in the chamber of his semi-automatic weapon.

As he followed, a gush of wind is detected through the 311 transmission, along with heavy breathing (which almost certainly implies that the watchman was running and in hot pursuit of the suspect). In a lower voice, the watchman utters the word, "fucking coons", then the 311 operator asked the watchman was he following him? The watchman replied affirmative. The operator informed him that was unnecessary and didn't need him to perform that task, to which the watchman replied ok. The watchman then disobeyed this command, continued to pursue and ultimately confronted the suspect. These remarks, along with the subsequent actions by the watchman, suggest willful, criminal and malicious intent. When interrogated after the shooting by the head investigator of the police department, the watchman stated that he wasn't following him; that he *was walking in his direction.* The detective replied that was indeed "following". The automobile door chimes signaling the opening of his car door, followed by heavy breathing which was picked up on the 311 call suggests that he was "running" in the same direction. The watchman obviously exaggerated the truth in this statement and contradicted his original statement, yet this detective came to the defense of the watchman in court.

MADAME K

The prosecution's proposed star witness and good friend of the suspect, Madame K, was like a bomb ready to explode in her original testimony. She was the last person to speak to the suspect, and was on the phone with him at the beginning of the conflict with the watchman. During her testimony, her courtroom decorum became an issue as she became defensive, to the point of rude at times. It became evident that the courtroom and the witness stand was the last place that she wanted to be. When she was informed that she would again have to take the stand after recess (after 3 hours of her testimony), she loudly exclaimed, what!? She gave the impression of a "double-talker", or a person who quickly (or not so quickly) and constantly contradicts their own statements, in the manner of a shrewd prevaricator and manipulator of information. When asked certain questions, many times she would pause and her eyes would roll upwards, as if to search for, or create, answers. Her testimony was probably perceived by the jury as non-credible, as she was apparently totally unprepared to take the witness stand.

She also appeared as though she were hiding something that she did not want to expose. Although she was the suspect's good friend since elementary school, she did not attend his funeral, issuing a harsh reply as to her reason for not going. In speculation, she may have encouraged the suspect to physically confront the man who was stalking him. Maybe her conscience wouldn't let her be truthful in front of the suspect's parents and the general public. Her testimony was that she told the suspect to *run* in his response to his stating to her that he was being followed by this creep-ass cracker. But even if that were the case, she can't be blamed. If the suspect did actually throw the first punch, he did it on his own despite her encouragement, but it begs the questions, why was it necessary that he throw the first punch? Or better still, why was the watchman that close to him? An additional question could be, how could the suspect have initiated the fight as the watchman suggests, while being stalked and talking on the phone at the same time? Madame K stated that while the suspect was on the phone with her, he stated to her that he was being followed by this creep-ass cracker. Subsequent to the verdict, a juror stated to a national news broadcast that the comment was not racist in her opinion, felt sorry for Madame K, that she did not make a good witness, and that this is the type of life that "they" live, in the environment that they live in, everyday life. This juror's remark basically categorizes, compares and contrasts her own culture to the culture of both the suspect and Madame K, as she repeatedly refers to "they" as a reference point. Of course the defense tried to rearrange these words to make the suspect look like the racist by the remark, but *the statement implies that he was being stalked by that person.* She basically painted them both with the same broad and biased paintbrush, and this may have affected her final thoughts prior to her input to the jury decision.

Another fact may be that Madame K may have listened to the accounts that lead to the homicide and aftermath take place, and may have become afraid to get involved. She also may have received death threats prior to the trial by the watchman's supporters, as he was rumored to be supported by various racial groups. Maybe she was persuaded not to testify in a pro-suspect manner. She confessed on the witness stand that she hid in the closet when talking to certain attorneys on the phone. What was she afraid of? Another question that needs to be asked is, why didn't the prosecution subpoena the various cell phone companies involved and reproduce a recording of the entire cell phone conversation between the suspect and Madame K (which may have revealed vital information if the telephone connection was still open after the shooting) to use as evidence? That phone call is a vital piece to the "invisible time frame".

Although branded as ignorant by the defense and one of the defense attorney's daughters, she was sharper than most reviews gave her credit. She was even humiliated and defamed on national TV. The president of the gated community and a good friend of the watchman referred to her as Precious, a sarcastic racial reference to the star of a black situation movie. Precious was the portrayal of an overweight, dark-complexioned teenager with mental aptitude problems. At times, it appeared she had no clue, but it became evident that she was very much aware, and understood perfectly the direction of the line of questioning by the defense. If she did "play dumb" while on the witness stand, it could be that she wanted to hide something. In fact,

Madame K was very astute, shrewd and her power of recall (previous days and dates of the week) was somewhat amazing at the beginning of her testimony, although the prosecution and the defense both had trouble deciphering what her truths were.

Her presence created a cultural difference in the courtroom that was as contrast as night and day. The defense lawyers seemed to have trouble following her dialect and language mannerisms. At one point, Madame K explained that she was once in a three-way with the suspect. In shock, the defense attorney's eyes and heads turned when she made that remark. She actually caught the whole courtroom off guard with the remark, as they were inclined, at first, to think that she was talking about sex. She was actually talking about a three-way telephone conversation that she had with the suspect and another friend. Both sides of the stand had trouble connecting with this bombshell of a witness, due to many of these cultural differences.

Although she may or may not have instigated the suspect to engage in a fight with the watchman, she did explain to the Court that she heard the cell phone hit the ground, following the remarks, get off me, get off me, what are you doing around here? She earlier stated that it sounded like the watchman shoved the suspect, causing his cell phone to fall in the grass. This act may be what initiated the physical confrontation. This study acknowledges these statements to be the absolute truth, but she was made into a buffoon by the defense, so as not to give her any credibility during the trial. These comments also dispute the statements made by the watchman that the subject jumped out of the bushes and sucker-punched him in the nose on his way back to his car. In fact, there were no bushes. The defense attorneys became very harsh about these and other statements made by Madame K, which she was made to repeat ad nauseum. Noticeably impatient to the point of frustrated by the barrage of heated questions, Madame K was ultimately discredited as the state's star witness. In one and a half years since the incident, the prosecution in this case did not properly prepare Madame K for the witness stand, as she appeared to be ill-advised, and it is not surprising that her important testimony was not properly presented. Madame K gave too many conflicting prior statements to lawyers and police, and her attitude and behavior on the witness stand bordered on shameful. She should have apologized to the family members of the deceased for wasting their time, because she did not help them and could have.

WHOSE VOICE WAS THAT?

Accenording to the defensive testimony, at least seven witnesses identified the last voice before the fatal shot as that of the watchman, including his family members. Upon his initial interrogation by the head detective who asked him was that his voice, the watchman originally stated that the voice *didn't even sound like him*, thereby denying the question. Not only that, the detective insisted that was his voice, maybe in anticipation of a self-defense trial. Maybe the watchman had a "macho-moment", through his perception of the audacity of the question, and momentarily forgot his plan. So proud of what he had just done, maybe he was telling the truth. He changed his story after being counseled by his attorneys. All of the witnesses who were called in behalf of the prosecution recognized and identified the final voice to be that of the suspect, and most were immediate relatives. Madame K also said that it was the suspect's voice, but her testimony was deemed less than credible by the jury throughout the trial.

In the opinion of the defense, and ultimately the jury, the cry for help and the obvious pleading for life belonged to the watchman, the guy with the gun. In analogy, this was a man, a hunter, who observed and followed his prey, armed with a 9mm semi-automatic handgun. Most hunters enjoy the sport for the delicacy/ food aspect; others hunt with a desire to collect trophies (i.e. antlers, skins, etc.) while others take pride in their marksmanship by making a "clean" kill. In most cases though, the prey doesn't usually attack the hunter, and the hunter doesn't usually cry for help. You also have to figure in speculation that even if the prey did attack the hunter, the hunter had it coming to him, survival of the fittest; because the prey was being stalked and was defending his own self-preservation. The prey would, in effect, "be standing his ground". Even a deer will attack if he is cornered. However, this is not an ordinary circumstance. Except for the defensive testimony in this case, this would normally be a rare occurrence.

The fact that the Court wouldn't allow parts of the testimony from the sound expert witness, who was subpoenaed to court to determine whose voice it was before the fatal shot, mandated further silence to the deceased suspect's side of the story. The prosecution should have also asked the expert to clarify the "fucking coons" remark (which was reproduced in a lower tone), giving the watchman's supporters a leeway to cloud that issue. In speculation, was the 311 tape doctored to make the remark sound lower than it originally was? It could be that the expert wasn't allowed to testify about the comment, and it never came up as a subject during the trial. However, the term was used by the watchman and it is interpreted as an angry racial slur; *a term usually made by the bigoted white person about black people in general.* Historically in America, the term "coons" is equivalent to the term, "niggers". According to the Court, the term was never stated, didn't exist and was never used, as the Court barred such testimony. The prosecution should have called for a mistrial.

The watchman's witnesses, close friends and contributors to his defense fund stated to the Court that they could tell it was his voice because, they said, they heard him scream before. They supposedly heard him whooping it up at and some kind of political rally and/ or football game. Other witnesses came to the defense of the watchman including two police officers, one of whom first interrogated him at the police station before he was let go. Question: How could these police officers know what the watchman's scream sounded like if they just met him upon his first arrest? If they didn't know what he sounded like, how could they testify in court that they believed that it was? These and other witnesses were all assumed to be credible at the least.

With only the parents, Madame K and the brother's testimony, it was up to the jury to interpret and determine who the final screams belonged to. The interpreter should have been able to determine who had more of a reason to yell for help, the guy who was being stalked or the guy with the gun. But let us imagine that the voice belonged to the teenaged suspect. If this is the suspect, doesn't it sound as if the watchman wanted to hear him beg for his life before he executed him; as in cold-blooded murder? After a 911 call was put through by a neighbor, the listener can hear continuous screaming and pleading for help as she was terrified throughout the duration of the call. She said the voice sounded like a young boy. The screaming lasted for about 45 seconds and suddenly stopped with the fatal shot. How long had the screaming been going on before the call was made? If this was, in fact, the teenaged suspect, then that was a death scream (or yell), and the proper charge should have been murder in the first degree, because the murder would have been premeditated for approximately 60 seconds before the watchman actually pulled the trigger. It would mean that he held the gun on him for that long. He had that much time to decide whether to shoot and kill a young boy. Together with the "fucking coons" remark, this would be a premeditated hate crime. This is the theory which precludes that the watchman did it for the worst of all reasons…because he wanted to.

In the opinion of this study, the prosecution provided weak evidence at the trial. Where were the blood-splatter experts who could explain the absence of blood on the watchman's jacket or pants, if he shot the suspect at such a close distance? The watchman was alleged to be at the bottom of the altercation with the suspect straddling him on top. If the suspect was on top, where are the grass stains on the knees of his pants, as it was raining? The human body is like a balloon filled with blood. If it is punctured by a bullet, blood will spray/ splatter. How is it that the watchman had none of the suspect's blood on his clothes or skin? Also, how could he fire a perfect 90 degree angle shot to the heart from his lying position In the "altercation"? How could he have drawn the gun that was holstered behind his back from that position? How is it that the deceased was lying face down in the grass, a good number of feet away from the sidewalk where the watchman insisted that his head was being bashed in while, at the same time, being bashed with the subject's fists who was also trying to take the gun from him? Why was there none of the watchman's DNA on the suspect's knuckles and hands, or abrasions on his fist from an alleged fight for that matter? If the suspect was reaching for his gun, where is his DNA or fingerprints on the pistol and/ or the holster? The 90 degree angle of the shot suggests that they were both standing at the time of the shot, and the lack of blood splatter on the watchman's jacket presupposes that he was at some distance, but with his arm extended and the gun right up to the suspect's chest at a 90-degree angle, as he begged for his life. It also suggests that he killed the suspect with one shot to a critical area, his heart.

How could the suspect have pounded him with his fists, bash his head against the sidewalk, cover both the watchman's nose and mouth, and also reach for his gun which was holstered behind his back, unless he had five hands? The prosecution did a poor to mediocre job at investigating these inconsistencies and more key points of evidence. With only the alleged non-credible statements made by Madame K, the final screams and pleas for help before the fatal shot were the suspect's only testimony, and only witness.

The watchman's defense basically overwhelmed and suffocated any strategy by the prosecution to prove that the voice was the deceased suspect, by the sheer number of witnesses who took the stand and declared that the voice was their boy's. Despite the fact that the watchman himself admitted to the police in his initial interrogation that the voice didn't even sound like him, he is overruled by his own character witnesses and the detective himself who insisted that *was* his voice, in preparation for trial. The prosecution had minimal evidence to suggest that it was the suspect's voice during the last minute of his life, and seemed to rely on the "common sense" of the jury, which in many cases takes precedence despite enormous amounts of evidence; that and the fact that you have a dead child who is unable to explain his side of the story. However, the jury believed the narrative and the evidence of the defense. In the opinion of this study, the facts outweigh the evidence for a watchman conviction. The most important evidence, besides the dead body and what would have been the suspect's actual testimony had he lived, is suppressed by the testimony of so-called friends of the watchman and the police officers, thereby silencing the deceased teenaged suspect. Without his voice, he was, in fact, on trial for his own murder.

STAND YOUR GROUND

"Stand your ground" law is one of the most archaic laws in American history. The law stems from the days of the wild west, when cowboys and other men were allowed to duel to the death via gunfight. The winner was the one who stood and lived after the culmination of the duel. In understanding this law, it appears evident that the participant (or killer) who shows up to testify in court is the winner, especially if there are no witnesses to testify against him. A one-on-one duel implies that each party has the right to claim, "stand your ground". If the person who initiates the conflict through words or action ultimately kills the person who dares to retaliate, he has the right to claim self-defense, even though he started the conflict. The killer is the winner. With the introduction of race, however, this law seems to take a different path.

In contrast, there is the case of a black woman from the state of Florida, who defended herself by shooting at a wall to instill fright in an approaching and menacing husband. He stated that he had six baby mamas and hit them all except one. The only mistake she made was not to kill him, because that allowed him to testify against her in court. She tried to apply the "stand your ground" law to her defense, however unsuccessfully, and received a 20-year sentence for her actions. Ironically and coincidentally, she was successfully prosecuted by the very same team of lawyers who showed incompetence in the prosecution of the watchman. The theme of justice and equality as it applies to the races will continue to diversify and raise questions in the American society, so long as laws such as these are allowed to exist. The law does not care who initiated the conflict and greatly enhances an individual's ability to use the law in search of a personal vendetta. The law is dangerous, ambiguous and primitive in nature. Thankfully, the woman was recently pardoned by the President.

The "stand your ground" law begs the question: Is there a double standard when it comes to the application of this law. Is this a "catch-22" law? Does the law uphold every self-defense allegation that it is applied to? Does a citizen have the right to stand his ground against a police officer or military person who is ready and poised to shoot at him, or is shooting at him, or does his change with race? If the watchman had killed a blond, blue-eyed white girl/ boy under the same conditions, does he get a "not guilty" verdict? If the races of the victim and the assailant were reversed, would it have taken six weeks for him to be formally charged with a homicide? A great criminal defense attorney explained that "race determines everything in the criminal justice system", and that "race is the prism through which people see things". Social inequality tends to plague the American legal system. In his debate with Stephen Douglas, Abraham Lincoln stated, "I am not nor ever have been in favor of bringing about in any way the social and political equality of the black and the white race…I as much as any other man am in favor of having the superior position assigned to the white race". In keeping up with "tradition", could these words by Lincoln be the basis of the watchman's non-arrest?

Another speculation is that the teenaged suspect was the guy that the watchman didn't want to let get away. Being that the suspect ran, the watchman had to chase after and catch up with him on foot *for the purpose of creating a scenario of self-defense in an area with no witnesses.* Was this law created for a situation like this, to facilitate the situation of whites, but not blacks? Is black life not equal to white life in the courtroom? Does this law make it "open season" on black males for twelve months a year? Was Rodney King the victim of police brutality or was he resisting arrest? Is this a law that allows you to kill black people and receive a "not guilty" verdict? Is this law a license to kill? What is meant by "looking at the world through rose-colored glasses"?

MADAME X

Developments since the trial have to do with the watchman's wife, Madame X, who has at this time filed for divorce, as well as the actions of the watchman himself. Among the irreconcilable differences that she filed in her divorce papers is that she claimed the watchman to be a selfish person who makes reckless decisions and feels invincible since the not guilty verdict. More recent is the incident at her father's household where he threatened her and her father with a gun and a knife, smashed a device that she was using to record his actions in an obvious attempt to destroy evidence, punched the father in the face, daring them both to step closer, as in prompting them for the purpose of shooting them; very much aware of the "stand your ground" law. She exclaimed to 911 that she was really scared, and didn't know what he was capable of, although no charges were filed. This incident was an obvious reaction by the watchman to the fact that she filed for divorce and explained to the national talk-show circuit about the wayward disposition of her unpredictable husband.

By striking her father and openly brandishing a weapon in a non-self-defensive manner, it is apparent that his respect and regard for other people (including significant others) is questionable. The police dismissed her charge as a domestic problem, however they continued to overlook and dismiss serious allegations against this person, who was obviously in need of some restraint and observation. Instead of remorse for the unnecessary shooting of a teenager, he appears to be looking toward areas of approval for his actions, as if this homicide was his moment of glory. This behavior may be the result of his continuing gun ownership, permit to carry and his "trophy" display, reflecting a sense of overconfidence and "invincibility" since the not guilty verdict was given.

Madame X also revealed that she and the watchman had an argument the night before he killed the teenaged suspect, which caused her to leave their home and stay with her father. Could the death of the suspect be a result of the residual anger, insecurity and/ or frustration that the watchman may have accumulated as a product from the argument with his wife the night before? Is he insecure about black men in general? Did he lose a few street fights in his career and as a result obtain a gun permit and purchase a pistol? Did he ventilate his anger and insecurity on an unarmed 16-year old black teenager because he was, in fact, black? He may have enjoyed killing the suspect. No way should this person be allowed to carry a firearm, but he is still on patrol. One police chief in the area said he would certainly consider the idea of revoking the watchman's gun permit, after noting his pattern of deviant behavior. Psychiatric intervention for the watchman should be of the first order.

This trial was also unique/ unusual by the fact that the defendant in a murder trial was rewarded and applauded for his actions from the beginning, and that many of the watchman's supporters had been donating cash to his website, apparently in an effort to uphold the "tradition" and defend him in the symbol of white supremacy. The only other conceivable alternative motive to this continuous funding would be too incredible to comprehend; that hundreds of thousands of dollars were being donated to a site that supports the victimization of teenage children. He was also honored by a local business establishment in an apparent celebration of the homicide and as a named celebrity for anti-black white racism; in the form of a cult hero.

Maybe the menacing of a white woman (his wife) and the physical assault on her father will begin to shed light on his true character. The racial element would possibly drop the watchman from the payroll now that he's attacking white people. If this case is not about race, then the teenager was killed for no reason at all, except that the watchman may be so psychotic that he did actually commit the homicide because he wanted to. What else could be the real motive to this unnecessary homicide? Was it maliciously impulsive? Although the teenager had not committed a crime, the watchman was triggered into action when he began to run, but since when is running a crime? Also, when did the watchman become a policeman?

PATHOLOGY AND FORENSICS

More recent developments since the trial ended have to do with the medical examiner that performed the autopsy on the teenaged suspect. He was fired from his position because he was ordered to resign and refused. During the trial, Dr. Z testified that he could not remember key facts related to the autopsy. As a result of his apparent "amnesia" on the witness stand, prosecutors have sought to terminate the doctor for poor performance during the testimony. Another attorney unrelated to the trial stated that the doctor took the majority of the blame for mistakes made in the state's case against the watchman. But was it actually the doctor's fault that the trial was lost by the prosecution? Was he a scapegoat?

Subsequent to this firing, the doctor has filed a lawsuit against the state in his behalf, for wrongful termination and ethnic discrimination. His lawyer made it clear that he was fired to take the blame for the prosecution's failure to convict the watchman, and that it was also a desired failure; a case willfully and intentionally lost because they were all biased against the teenage suspect. Not only that, the suspect got what he deserved, according to the doctor's interpretation of the attitude of the prosecution. His attorney stated that the doctor was given a gag order not to say things relevant to the case in support of the suspect. It became obvious to the viewer that the doctor was purposely withholding crucial information about the autopsy; a medical school graduate with short-term memory loss. One of his recent admissions was that he had scientific evidence that there was *no way the suspect could have been on top of the watchman*, and that the suspect was not the aggressor of the altercation, but that prosecutors never asked him "leading" questions that would have allowed him to explain his full diagnosis of the dead body, and the crime scene would have favored a conviction. One of the key points of evidence is *the trajectory of blood flow from the watchman's head wounds ran toward his face*, as opposed to the rear of his head as it should have if he was on the bottom of the altercation, but the prosecutors never asked him questions that were crucial or germane to this aspect of the case. Another key point is that the amount of marijuana that was found in the teenager's system would have made him less aggressive. One attorney stated that the doctor was blocked by the prosecution, as he had 7 points he wanted to make during the trial. The doctor stated that the prosecution investigators usually come in to review the autopsy, take notes, ask questions, etc., but in this instance, they said that this was a straightforward case of self-defense. They looked at the case as being over, so they threw it.

A noted criminal forensics expert is rumored to have testified in behalf of the defense, hired at the rate of $8,000/ hr. for his time. Many legal analysts inferred that the professional testimony and reputation of this expert is what sealed the not guilty verdict for the watchman.

Once again, was the doctor an original piece to his puzzle? His odd testimony was that he could not remember facts of the case pertaining to the autopsy, however *he totally recalled the entire autopsy procedure coincidental with his termination.* He is regarded as an excellent medical examiner and as a result he, himself, is shocked because of his own dismissal. It is in the opinion of this study that he was ordered to withhold key evidence from the trial in order to increase the possibility of an acquittal. Was this a pre-arranged verdict? Much of the normal police procedure to a homicide was either intentionally overlooked and/ or basically left out of the process; actions that enhanced the watchman's chances at a possible acquittal. Based on these assumptions and the doctor's recent statements, these components are examples of legal improprieties.

NEW DEVELOPMENTS

The truth about the watchman has surfaced through the revelations of the doctor and his ex-wife, Madame X. Even though she and her father previously dropped all charges against him, she regrets not filing charges against him for his most recent episode at the father's house. She testified that she is basically afraid of him and his recent behavior. She also stated that has doubts as to his innocence in the slaying of the teenaged suspect. Her statements imply that the watchman was not defending himself when he shot and killed the teenager. What was his true reason for shooting him? Police were recently called to his mother-in-law's house because she accused him of stealing furniture and other property. Although this charge was dismissed as a domestic problem, the authorities appear to be very lenient and aversive when it comes to the handling of the watchman. Why does the law keep turning a "blind eye" to his misdeeds? The watchman left a bullet-riddled target on the living room wall of their home, after she asked him to move out. It was found after she returned home from a TV show to discuss the wayward character and behavior of her now-infamous husband. She stated to her lawyers, look at the message he sent me.

Most of the speculation in this study focused on (1) the possibility that the watchman may have committed a race-hate crime and (2) that there was a note of corruption in the legal process that was performed. The recent testimonies of these two figures (Madame X and the doctor) in related cases has unraveled a series of new revelations that are not surprising and are congruent with this study, as writing began with the verdict and it is now 4 years later. Madame X implied that law enforcement officials dictated her decision not to file charges on her husband and in such a manner as to protect him; and in a manner similar to the jury instructions that coerced the six women to set the watchman free. Regardless that this trial should never be reopened through appeal, and based on the statements by the doctor, something should be said as to legal misconduct and corruption of justice. If these revelations are accurate, they may involve many high-ranking government officials. New charges of kidnap and false arrest, by the fact that he (1) illegally detained the suspect (2) confined him to an area (3) made a false citizen's arrest without there being a crime committed. In speculation, his satisfaction could have come from what he thought would be an approval from the police department for this detainment-turned -homicide, in his warped dream of becoming a police officer. Reckless endangerment, aggravated child abuse, and endangering the welfare of a minor should also be considered.

It is the opinion of this study that the watchman either had a vendetta to settle, as he waited patiently in his car as the subject approached, simultaneous with *an instant call, upon sight of the suspect,* to 311 in an effort to pre-disclose his self-defense statement, or that he hunted the teenager as a sport or game; the same as a hunter who goes after and ultimately "bags" a deer. Through a hunter's perception, he hunted an animal that he felt didn't deserve as much of a right to live as he. It was game that he specified as prey through learned symbols and values, game that eluded him, game that frustrated him and game that he became angry with. It appears that the ultimate killing and display of the teenaged suspect's body was the "trophy" that he sought all along; not to mention the high dollar figure that he received in an auction for the weapon that he used in the homicide, a weapon he calls a piece of American history. On the tail end of an argument with his wife the night before, it appears that he took out his aggression on a black kid because he was black, didn't like the way he looked or acted, and at the same time aspired to make others see the "threat" that he saw via the 311 call. Whether any of the charges or accusations against him "fit" the incident that he provoked, he should have been arrested for "something", as testified by major public opinion.

The watchman may have enjoyed killing the teenaged suspect. He was gushing with pride when a police officer pulled him over, and asked the officer if he recognized who he was. His wife stated that he celebrated the verdict without her, describing it as a victory tour. A victory tour? What was he celebrating, a young kid's death that he caused? Did the prosecution really believe that the teenager got what he deserved? Is this an idea that is in the "best interests of the ruling class", as stated by the tenets of conflict theory in sociology. What did he do to deserve death? Why did he deserve death if the watchman could have avoided his actions, knowing he was armed? Why didn't the jury take into consideration that the watchman initiated the whole situation, or give any consideration to the fact that the teenager had a right to stand HIS ground? Was the symbol and meaning of the deceased teenager's death instrumental in the promotion of social instability subsequent to the incident? Was this case politicized by political parties for the purpose of winning elections?

Did the watchman profile the teenager as belonging to a social group? Sociologists define a social group as a collection of individuals who share certain characteristics, interact and share a common identity. Through his own learned value system, the adjectives that he used to describe the teenager, looks like he's up to no good, he's wearing a hoodie, on drugs or something, and he's a black male warrant the profile of a black criminal. With the description of the teenager by the use of these terms, he is also raising "red flags" into the value systems of the dispatch operator who would then instill them into the police who were to arrive at the scene first, much like the officers who arrived first in the Tamir Rice case; in a series of transmitted values and as a way of biasing the whole legal process in his favor.

A noted news anchor stated that the hoodie was as much responsible for the kid's death as the killer was, insisting that this is the common dress that you observe on surveillance tapes when black men are committing crimes. It is also the common dress of basically every adult and child in North America, including Eskimos, for the purpose of keeping their head warm. Does the hoodie take on special significance and connotations when it is worn by a black male? Hoodies are also worn by the Ku Klux Klan. Should black individuals feel self-conscious when wearing a hoodie in American society? The reporter insisted that he was trying to save lives amidst the uproar of this case. He insisted that they were risking their lives because many people (including police) are negative and racially-aggressive. If all accounts of these new developments are true, then the verdict that acquitted the watchman should be included as one of the worst decisions in United States judicial history, along with the verdict that set free the killers of Emmett Till.

Supportive of these stereotypical depictions are the teenaged suspect's picture on shooting targets that one police officer brought in for training purposes. One has to wonder how much did the watchman impress law enforcement officials throughout the country with his act. The targets had a hooded silhouette of the perpetrator as the face of the target. The officer was instantly discharged for his lack of sensitivity. Top brass immediately followed with a deep apology to the teenager's family, insisting that the act of the officer was intolerable. The officer defended his actions by stating what was done to him was out of political correctness. What else can be said about this situation except that it appears to be "open season" on black males. Are cops trained to suspect, shoot and kill innocent black people through conditioning and targets such as these? Would the insertion of a white face be acceptable for the front of police gun targets? Were these targets especially created as instruments in which to train adults in the new civil war against children? The watchman has become a cultural icon, cult hero and the poster boy for white racism and gun rights activists. He is a hero to many groups that do not even seem to fathom the grief that the teenager's family and a great portion of the American society have endured, by the unnecessary death of their child.

OPPOSING IDEOLOGIES

The lead investigator told the watchman during the first interview after the shooting that this wasn't just any kid…he was a good kid with a future…wanted to be a rocket scientist. The officer is a professional at his job and probably investigated numerous crimes before and since the tragic incident, probably knew better than anyone what the nature of the crime was that he had before him; however his testimony that he believed it was the watchman's voice before the fatal gunshot isn't congruent with his intelligence. The watchman basically admitted to him that it wasn't his voice during a macho moment, forgetting his plan. Taking notice of the original over-zealous pursuit, he stated at the outset that the watchman appeared anxious to get the bad guy. For two weeks, the State Attorney's Office denied his original request to arrest the watchman for manslaughter; and it would be four additional weeks before he was officially arrested for the crime of murder. One DNA analyst determined that it may not have been a big scuffle by the fact that the wounds to the watchman were small and insignificant. The EMT on the scene determined that his injuries were minor and did not warrant hospitalization. The EMT also pronounced the teenager dead.

There is an enormous sense of pride and greatness that emanated from the black struggle in the United States. Frederick Douglas once stated that, "if there were no struggle, there would be no progress". The American black culture that lived during the 1960's felt that enthusiasm all throughout their conscience, as blacks were finally making advances in mainstream society, and were now becoming very assertive and recognized through popular culture. There was anger and outrage as black leaders (i.e. Stokely Carmichael , Martin Luther King, Malcolm X, Adam Powell, Eldridge Cleaver, Muhammad Ali, H. Rap Brown, etc.) spoke with fiery dialect to reflect the intolerance and disgust that people felt, as racism, segregation, inequality and civil rights were major issues of the day. Black children and young adults today don't seem to acknowledge the black revolution of the 50's and 60's, and this may be due to the techniques of the American educational system that doesn't include the whole referendum of black achievements and major struggles of the past/ recent past in their social studies books. American history contains many black American tragedies and achievements, and something every American can learn from. The tragedy of Emmett Till is an example of this non-inclusion, as he is basically unmentioned in the social studies texts. By the same token, so are Lewis Latimer, Patricia Bath and Garrett Morgan, among others.

Truthfully, everyone knows what happened that night, just like they know what happened to Emmett Till, despite the verdict and whether or not it will ever be proven. The murderers of Emmett Till admitted with great description and gave reasons as to what they had done to the child in an interview with Look Magazine shortly after the trial was over. They know a young man's life has been taken for basically no reason at all, except maybe racial hatred or because he was profiled as a suspicious black character, which is basically the same thing. Furthermore, they know through experience that white life is more valued than black life in the society, and this type of racial injustice has plagued the American legal system historically. Finally, they know the whole incident could have been avoided and that the watchman was acquitted, as one juror stated a day late and a dollar short. There were collective millions of whites, Asians, Hispanics Jews, Indians, Christians, etc. who were all marching together to protest the verdict and pay tribute to the teenager, even overseas. Their numbers alone seemed to indicate that injustice had been done. Since the verdict, many ex-watchman supporters have switched sentiments because they know the truth in their heart. Many of the white (and other) protesters have black children, grandchildren, nieces, nephews and other relatives of color. If the watchman profiled and attacked the teenager because of his color, these people are responding to that issue as well. In the opinion of this study, the prosecution presented their case but left out many vital elements, and didn't properly prepare key witnesses. What about the fact that the watchman referred to blacks as "fucking coons" as he was chasing the suspect? Also, the fact that that he set up 311 and apparently premeditated as to what he was about to do, and that is kill someone who allegedly appeared "suspicious" to him. If you look closely at the watchman's six assorted mug shots, *he looks more sinister than anyone else involved*. It appears evident that he would never have followed the suspect if he didn't have that gun, which he was anxious to use, along with his academic training for a legal self-defense claim. Maybe his primary goal in purchasing a gun was to kill a person, preferably a black person, and maybe this need grew from the day he received the gun permit and bought the gun, as it took him only two years to accomplish the feat of killing someone. It also took only five months after he started the neighborhood watch program to kill someone. Could this be the reason that he wanted to start the program?

Right after the incident, major talk-show hosts and race-baiters quickly endorsed the watchman, over-defended him to their ultra-conservative audiences, and quickly shunned anyone who spoke up for the teenager on their highly acclaimed conservative talk/radio/television shows. It was as though they turned the incident into a morality play of good vs. evil; good being synonymous with white (or the watchman). The teenager was here tagged as a "thug" and a "hoodlum", and the watchman was openly described as a mentor to black children, among other praising accolades by many of these conservatives. What ever happened to those children anyway? Were there any? Is the word "thug", as it is constantly applied to the character of the suspect, a code word for the term, "nigger"? Right from the beginning, the watchman's token character witness and a perceived black "Uncle Tom" by a national TV audience defended his use of the word "coons". The witness said that the phrase is used as a term of endearment.

The reference, "fucking coons", was discussed and analyzed by various reporters. The term was totally denied and unrecognized by the character witness and other watchman supporters, even though the witness told them that term coon-ass was used by the natives of Louisiana, and that his daughter told him that the phrase is used as a "term of endearment". The witness stated that it sounded like 'goons' when the actual comment was replayed to him. Unwittingly, when the witness stated the coon-ass remark, he actually acknowledged that he did, in fact, hear the word "coon" in the comment. Did he actually believe that the watchman would have used a term of endearment during his armed pursuit of a guy that he profiled as a menacing black criminal? The rules of the Court turned "coons" into "punks" as the replacement word for what was really said. The lead investigator asked the watchman about the remark in the first interrogation, and although it was brushed off as a topic, the detective knew what he heard. He even asked the watchman if he were racist, in response to the remark. Just like Rodney King, where many viewed his beating as "resisting arrest" as opposed to police brutality; in this case, supporters of the defense have chosen not to pay attention to phonics. Most individuals pay attention to, have trust and belief in their own eyes and ears. A hard "C" does not sound like a hard "P" or "G"; and an "N" does not sound like a hard "K". "Coons" is a phonetically different word and doesn't sound like "punks" or "goons". However, in the courtroom the word "punks" was the accepted replacement word. The question becomes, why didn't the Court accept the actual word that was used?

The watchman was caught in a few lies. His original bail was revoked by the first judge on the case, because he and his wife lied about funding that he received through donations, and by not turning in a passport. The watchman was recalled to prison, bail revoked and reset. He and his wife were subsequently recorded talking in code about the transference of finances over a jailhouse telephone. As a consequence, his wife was implicated and ultimately convicted for lying to a bail hearing about their finances. The judge was eventually asked to step down after an appeal was made by the defense. Another lie was told during an exclusive interview when he described the suspect as skipping away, as opposed to running away, like he originally told the 311 operator. The exaggeration of this truth was to make it appear that the suspect wasn't running that fast or out of fear of him. During the 311 call, he sounded anxious to apprehend this suspicious black guy, and was requesting police assistance. It appears that the watchman made the 311 call as soon as he made visual contact with the suspect, while sitting in his car, and began to follow the suspect as the suspect walked past his car. When the suspect began to run, the watchman stopped his car and began a foot pursuit. The wind through the watchman's cellphone doesn't suggest "skipping" by either party. He told the arresting officer that he wasn't following him, but that he was walking in the same direction. The officer told him that was, in fact, following. He told the officer that the kid was in his late teens, but could not tell how old he was when interviewed on a talk-show later. There were many inconsistencies in the watchman's pre-trial statements to the police and subsequent interviewers. When asked if he regrets his decision to kill the teenager and would he have done things differently if given the chance, he replied no, as he considered it a Divine plan. Is that his testimony? Does he have no remorse for his actions? He is, in effect, stating that he would again profile the young black "suspect" and again engage in a deadly encounter with the youth.

Another question has also never been explained. How is it that the first person who arrived at the shooting scene just happen to arrive with a camera and take perfect photographs of the watchman's injuries right after a homicide has taken place? Very unusual. Natural shock would be a legitimate reaction, but posing for photographs suggests that the incident may have been pre-cognitive. In speculation, did the photographer, himself, inflict the injuries on the watchman before the police arrived, maybe at the request of the watchman, one might ask? Self-inflicted injuries were also never brought up as a topic by the prosecution, and it should have been. The questionable blood flow direction of the watchman's head wounds was never taken into account, as blood flowed toward the front of his head/ face as opposed to a rear flow if the watchman was lying on his back. The half-smile/ smirk on the watchman's face speaks a million words. Another photograph of interest is the confident wink after the not guilty verdict was read, suggesting anything but. The photograph does not give the impression of innocence. Photographs and audio speak aloud in key moments. Jail phone call recordings released by the prosecutor indicated how his wife worried about his safety during transportation from jail. He indicated that he had his hoodie with him and no one would recognize him, followed by his burst of laughter. Not exactly a sign of innocence or remorse.

In speculation, the lacerations on the watchman's head could have been self-inflicted. Critical questions such as these were never explored. This study also speculates the question, did the prosecution demonstrate willful incompetence in their development of this case? They could have also charged the watchman with false imprisonment, kidnapping, reckless endangerment, aggravated child abuse, endangering the welfare of a minor and wrongful death. One author stated that self-defense is not a defense to false imprisonment. No crime had been committed. The prosecution charged the watchman with a crime that gave him an out. He had the opportunity not only to use "stand your ground" as a defense, but also allowed him not to take the witness stand; all the while discrediting the prosecution and the character of the teenager.

Prior to the trial, many legal news insiders discussed the possibility that the watchman was being overcharged (murder 1st degree) because the weight of reasonable doubt could easily overturn the case in his favor. Others would argue that he was undercharged with respect to the other crimes he committed. Had the prosecution been able to prove that the final voice was the teenager, murder in the first degree would have been appropriate, because the murder would have been premeditated for over 60 seconds of the teenager pleading for his life. Had the prosecution charged the watchman with these other crimes, this would have forced him to take the witness stand and would have thrown out the marijuana usage claim, and tainted cellphone messages. Could the verdict have been the result of an ongoing power struggle between the two major political parties in that state, rather than the actual guilt associated with this trial? According to one juror, the jury instructions were what set the watchman free, despite her opposition. Another juror also stated that the Court left her with no other verdict. The jury instructions practically called for a not guilty decision; a decision declared in the name of conservative (right-wing) philosophy and white supremacy, to many.

A SPECULATION AS TO WHY

Maybe due to the educational systems throughout the country, black youth born in the 80's and later do not fully understand and/ or identify with the black struggle for civil rights and equality of the 50's and 60's (and prior). Much black history has always been eliminated from the schoolbooks of schoolchildren, or included only as a footnote. The verdict that cleared the watchman of murder should awaken a mass of these children and have them do research, as well it should. Black history in America is American history. Where once it was taboo, as well as dangerous, for black men to date white women, it is now a common occurrence, along with mulatto offspring. Not only that, blacks and whites share the same educational facilities, work facilities, social events and interact with each other throughout daily life in modern-day America. The racial element within the country still exists however, and its ugly head re-emerges periodically.

A short article in a major NY newspaper reported that an ex-officer was fired for statements he made on Facebook, expressing that another thug was dead, in an expression of obvious indifference to the death of the teenager; demonstrated pleasure after the verdict. He was fired for his lack of political correctness, especially coming from an ex-law enforcement official. There are many others who label the teenager a "thug" and a "gangster", and they usually speak from a conservative point of view. The fact is that he was doing nothing wrong prior to the incident and had no criminal record. In fact, many have described him as quiet and laid back; an athlete. Why was the watchman supported by, and made a symbol of the racist and conservative element/ attitudes of so many Americans from the outset of the shooting? It's like they didn't care if the shooting was just or unjust; they were applauding the act itself; of killing a black person.

The death of the teenager should serve as a wake-up call to the black youth of America today that are concerned about this verdict, and give them a sense and feel of what the black struggle in this country is all about. It is a happening; a movement rooted in history and a state of mind that is still present. If you are outraged at the watchman verdict, then you feel the pain and anger of the 1950's and 60's. You are angry about injustice and outraged at what happened to Emmett Till, as well as the one-hour jury deliberation that set the killers free. You understand why Rosa Parks refused to give up her seat in a Birmingham city bus to a white man in 1955. You understand with passion why Martin Luther King led the March on Washington in 1963, and the fury behind the outrage of his assassination in 1968. You are shocked and bitterly angry at the racially-motivated bombing of an Alabama church that killed four young black girls (ages 14, 14, 14, and 11). You are completely outraged by such an extreme act; an act that was done by a racially-negative social group in direct reaction to the speech by MLK at the

March on Washington two weeks earlier in 1963, as a racial reaction made in direct symbolism. The conspirators of this crime were also acquitted due to key evidence that was intentionally not released by the Justice Department in 1963. You understand that poor socioeconomic conditions and inequality led to the disastrous Watts riot of 1965. You angrily understand why Muhammad Ali refused to be drafted into the US Army in 1967, and you can openly defend his disobedience. Why fight and risk your life for a country that refuses to acknowledge your existence, denies you equality, denies you opportunity, denies you justice and calls you "nigger" like that is your name? By the same token, why fight against a country that never did these things to you? You hold your head up and you are proud of the distinguished black athletes on the 1968 Olympics, especially Tommie Smith and John Carlos, who raised their black-fisted gloves to the sky on the winner's podium while the national anthem was being played. Even though they were stripped of their medals, suspended from the Games and made to evacuate the Olympic host city (Mexico City), theirs was a symbol of black pride, as well as a symbol of black defiance and a reaction to the condition of black people in America, repeated through the modern symbol of Colin Kapernick. Through role identification and the media, they were able to send an electronic message to the American government in behalf of millions of people who were determined to abolish racism, social inequality and mistreatment. Although it took much pain and sacrifice to get to the year 2017, social change seems to be taking even longer.

Many try to compare the verdict given to NFL great OJ Simpson to the verdict given to the watchman. There was outrage after both verdicts, however white American outrage was predominant after the "not guilty" verdict that was given to Simpson, for the murder of two white people, including his wife. The outrage stems from the imagined audacity of a black man to kill a white woman (or man) in America, for black life was always deemed unimportant when compared to white life. As stated by Lincoln, "...There must be the position of inferior and superior...there is a physical difference which forbids the two races living together on terms of social and political equality." Such an act that OJ was alleged to have done has historically been interpreted as more than murder, and usually followed up with a murderous lynch mob; in the same manner of feelings and outrage that white people felt against the notorious, yet infamous, Nat Turner, when scores of innocent slaves were killed as a result of his murderous escapade of slaveowners and their families, and used to demonstrate a deterrent to other blacks as to the nature of his crimes.

Photographs of OJ Simpson on the cover of national magazines made his facial skin to appear "darker" than usual; altering the hue of his complexion to blackness, in the name of all things black are bad, and all things white are good. Even after the trial was over and the verdict was given, it was not accepted. White American society felt injustice and wanted to get even with this presumed black murderer of white people; and although he was found not guilty, his punishment became a national "obligation". He lost a fortune in civil court due to these murders and was incarcerated for a matter that is directly related to the decision from the criminal court. Throughout the centuries, this type of action was always among the worst that a black man could commit (or even be accused of committing) in America, and in the Old South the punishment would have been more than harsh, more than torture, probably fatal and vicious regardless of any evidence or verdict. Had this been the case with the watchman (killing a white woman), this study predicts that his fate would have been a lot different than the one he received, and that he would not have been assigned the role of the white person, or "establishment representative", as he was in this case.

Racism in modern America is not the oppressive force that it once was in the not-too-distant-past. Whites and blacks go to school together, use the same facilities, work together, eat together, vote together, procreate together, play together, pray together and interact on a daily basis in most cities and towns. However, there are institutional spheres among whites, many of which have to do with race and class and never meant to be infiltrated. The American golf industry was recently among these institutions that were only open to a restricted public. Much of it had to do with racial hatred, yet it greatly has to do with the fact that many whites just do not want to co-mingle or interact with blacks on every level and in every institution. Some of these institutions are "sacred" to many of these whites and meant to be kept that way, many times even barring other whites. Ex-President Obama is disliked by a large public because he is black and was able to penetrate some of those spheres/ circles; among those include the enclosed perimeter surrounding the United States presidency, as well as the institution of that which is the President of the United States.

It is certain that many executives' and CEO's affairs, private parties and meetings aren't always racially inclusive despite class. Most of these affairs probably include only selected members of the society. It is almost certain that the ex-President could tell you firsthand that there are many institutional spheres that even he cannot penetrate despite his rank in government, and the most absurd part of it all is that it has to do with his skin color. Separation by class, religion and/ or skin color represents the real institutions of racism in society. They are a reflection of what the outer society aspires to be in theory, as most members of society aspire to have a higher socioeconomic status. The outer society may also wish to be closer to God, however are denied membership to certain religions. Many women believe that they would want to mingle, socialize and interact within circles that include the likes of Paris Hilton, Kim Kardashian, Georgina Bloomberg and other rich celebrities for example. However, it becomes impossible to sit at the same table with the high-rollers when you can't meet the minimum bet.

Although blacks have fought for this country and played a major role in all the wars, have made many great accomplishments and contributions in the arts and sciences, including inventions, medicine, medical equipment, positions in government, and were greatly instrumental in the historic building of this nation, these achievements are not reflected in the conscience of "Americanism". They are also not reflected in the modern job market of modern mainstream America. Opportunities are limited and unemployment is high in the black communities of the United States. Institutional (systemic) racism is an active social device that is used to accomplish this end. Since slavery/ free labor came to an end, blacks are not the work force they once were because of machines and technology. Quotas (or "tokenism") are also among the modern tools that are used in this regard. In effect, lack of employment and skills among the sorted out leads to negative social conditions and crime. The American penal institutions have picked up the slack and reaped the profits/ benefits of free labor since emancipation, and black men and women have routinely made up the greatest proportion of the inmates/ residents at these institutions.

There are many spheres in American society that certain whites do not ever want infiltrated by race or ethnicity, even If it's by the ex-President of the United States; even if it's by Tiger Woods, the most visible black man to ever penetrate the world of PGA Golf and golf itself in America, becoming one of the all-time championship greats at a young age; even if it's by Eric Holder, the first black Attorney General; even if it's by Judge Clarence Thomas, the second black person ever to be appointed as a Justice on the United States Supreme Court or Dr. Ben Carson, the first surgeon in international history to successfully separate cranially conjoined twins; even if it's Barry Bonds, the greatest home run hitter in major league baseball history, the list goes on. The last two centuries have seen a lot of "firsts" when it comes to black achievements, and those achievements should not be downplayed. They should act as an incentive to universal achieving, but much too often these great figures are poisoned by the pen and the media.

ETCETERA

The mother of the teenaged suspect became concerned that the media and the defenders/ supporters of the watchman were trying to destroy her deceased son's reputation by smearing his character, labeling him a "thug" and a "delinquent". This is the area that the conservative viewpoint tends to exaggerate in their negatively-descriptive characterizations of the black teenager. It is feed for steadfast opinions that desire to uphold and defend pre-existing values of American culture over human life; delivered and distributed by the conservative pop-culture stars of the media. The ill-conceived mediated character of the teenager weighed heavily in the jury decision and it was determined by one juror that the kid was responsible for his own demise, never taking into consideration that he was being stalked, or the responsibility that the stalker had for his death. Her reasoning was that the watchman became upset with all the recent burglaries at the complex and reached a tolerance point at the time of the killing, becoming displaced, going above and beyond what he should have. With that reasoning, she excuses the watchman for going over the top of what he should have, as in, "hey, it happens". *Doesn't above and beyond suggest guilt?*

Big hoopla/ eyebrows raised when the watchman went to visit the factory where the actual weapon was manufactured. Apologists representing the watchman's attorney staff were highly regretful that he would take this action, barely one month after the verdict. Much can be perceived by the demonstrative behavior and decisions that the watchman has made since the verdict, as also evident by the justifiable outrage of the attorney staff who facilitated his acquittal. The totality of this event, including a viral photograph of a smiling watchman shaking hands with the also smiling gun factory representative is an absolute symbol of mockery to the death of the teenager.

Not long after the verdict, the watchman takes on new notoriety and demonstrations of mental instability, which had resurfaced through an altercation at the home of his new girlfriend. The usual choking, gun menacing, destruction of property and ultimately barricading himself in the house before the police arrive routine that we have seen before with this person. This time, police confiscated an array of weapons and ammunition. Could the watchman be obsessed with guns and violence? Outrageous is the fact that one of the weapons was an AR-15 assault weapon, an exact duplicate of the same weapons that were used in the massacre incidents in Connecticut and Washington, DC; making one imagine what fascinated him about those incidents to the point that he bought an identical weapon of the same caliber. Both of the massacre incidents in Connecticut and Washington (the one in DC took place after the verdict) were recent incidents. Was he fascinated by the capability of the weapon? Was he envious of all the media attention and notoriety that those killers received for their misdeeds and the impact that it had on society, or does he reasonably fear social repercussions as a result of the incident and the verdict? Why would he buy weapons of such magnitude unless he envisioned killing scores of people? Hopefully, this will be the incident where the symbol of tradition will take a back seat to the more important issue of public safety. As an infamous cultural icon and the "establishment representative" for conservatives and racists, the symbol of the watchman must succumb and must deteriorate in the eyes of his supporters. The impact of his acquittal has set a bad precedent in society, as noted by the repeated racial incidents and the social disarray that has followed the verdict up until the year 2017.

For the first time in any of the watchman's police-related incidents, there does appear to be a change in the conservative viewpoint towards this individual. Despite the quick endorsements by radio/ tv personalities, the same personalities don't appear to want to touch the most recent revelations concurrent with the misfit character of the watchman, as his most recent actions have left them with "egg on their faces". All of a sudden, this recent incident involving his Caucasian girlfriend appears to exemplify his true character, and is causing reluctant others to agree that this individual may actually be, in fact, a danger to society. Maybe we should all be thankful that she is Caucasian, because only at this point is he receiving the proper attention and become identified as a possible menace to the overall society; and in the minds of both sides of the deceased teenager argument. If the society can somehow come to an agreement about the verdict given to the watchman in the area of appeal, unlike the Emmett Till verdict, the problem of social inequality as it exists in the American courtroom would simultaneously take a step in the right direction in as far as making an attempt to fixing the problem; and an intelligent method toward the desired goal of structural functionalism: the return of "social equilibrium".

EPILOGUE

The Court was right. This case should have not been about race, but because of the way the watchman committed this homicide, the racial overtones were overwhelming. Extreme racism is a form of insanity, as in the case of Adolf Hitler, and the act of the watchman falls within this realm beginning with the term "fucking coons". The only non-white juror stated that the watchman got away with murder. She originally voted for the murder charge, but was ultimately influenced by the other jurors and the so-called rules of deliberation; rules of which were suspect in this trial.

Race is, however, a minor point to the case when it is overshadowed by something of much greater importance. The case is really more about our children and their understanding of life. What do we say to them? What kind of world do we want them to live in? How do we protect them when we are the ones who are, in fact, killing them? Beginning with the use of alcohol, tobacco, drugs and abortion, are we aware that this activity affects the brain of a fetus, and greatly shapes the behavior and health of that child in later life? Do we care about them? Are "crack children" (from birth) more violent than others, and responsible for the high black-on-black murder and crime rates in this nation? Now they have sleeping pills that parents can administer to children. Do our infants and children really annoy us that much? What's next?

Kids are consumed by drugs and alcohol in a manner somewhat relative to the government's pacification of the American Indians, with respect to alcohol. The Indians were given liquor in exchange, and as a remedy, for all that was lost in their world, and still are restricted to reservations within the American society. Many of these kids later can't acquire or maintain suitable employment because of failed drug and alcohol tests. Moreover, how many kids are dying as a result of alcohol and/ or drugs? What caused a father, Eric Lehtinen of Washington State, to inject his four-year old son with heroin? What about the many cases of child abuse (some more extreme than others), child slavery, and people in trusted positions like Jerry Sandusky? What did those children in Newtown, Connecticut, those babies, ever do to anyone? Especially horrendous is that these murders happened less than two weeks before the Christmas holiday. Why are we issuing guns and gun permits to insane people? Are they insane at the time of purchase and being issued these items, or do they grow progressively psychotic with each day of owning both a gun and a permit? Does owning both a gun and a permit to shoot give them new confidence? It only took the watchman two years after he purchased the gun, and five months after he started the watch program, to shoot and kill someone with it. Prior to that, he never killed anyone before. Does this psychosis or psychotic progression also happen to certain cops and/ or other armed servicemen who eventually kill innocent people of color?

Do certain people desire to use their guns on something other than paper targets, bottles and tin cans after a while? Shouldn't there be a periodic mental evaluation of gun owners with permits? Is the over-manufacturing of guns a method that the government uses to curb the population, especially in the minority communities? Should the Second Amendment be revisited? These are questions that have gone unanswered. Can they even be asked? The whole incident has evolved into something greater now. The saga of the deceased teen was figuratively a "seed" that has already grown into a vast sea of awareness, and has ultimately broken a dam revealing many congruent and alternative social concerns surrounding the problem. The only answer is to come to a solution, in the way of prevention.

Recently in NYC, Judge Shira Scheindlin (who should be applauded) ruled that the "stop and frisk" police method is unconstitutional because black and Hispanic males were being stopped more frequently (90%) than any other race, and that 98.5% of these "stops" resulted in the humiliation, embarrassment and indignation of innocent people when no weapon was found. Scheindlin insisted that police relied on a policy of "indirect racial profiling" which led cops to stop "blacks and Hispanics who would not have been stopped if they were white" (Democracy Now, 11/6/13). Mayor Bloomberg of NYC argued that these stops resulted in the removal of an enormous amount of guns from the streets, resulting in lower murder rates since he took office. In response to Bloomberg, another question of this study becomes, "Besides adding more ethnic and black individuals to the criminal database which negatively affects their chances and opportunities at current and future career employment, what is the real purpose of taking guns off the street ("stop and frisk", discretionary buybacks, etc.) and *the gun companies, in turn, manufacture an exponential amount more weapons to put back on the streets?"* This only accomplishes the feat of removing older more dysfunctional weapons and replacing them with newer, highly functional and more accurate ones. This idea is comparable to filling up a bucket that has holes.

After the massacre in Connecticut, the President tried to push legislation before Congress to pass a "gun reform" bill in response to the tragedy at the Sandy Hook Elementary School, but Congress and the NRA wouldn't budge, despite the magnitude of the child massacre and thereby voted the bill down; as the anti-Obama element in Congress was strong. The President called it a "shameful day in Washington". One shooting survivor, Patricia Maisch said that Congress "had no soul…no compassion". Overall, in the larger scheme it is the adults who are to blame, and because of their negligence and stubbornness, as well as stupidity, our children are being murdered.

Think about the mother, Nancy Lanza, who gave her 20-year old child, Adam Lanza, an introvert who didn't have a criminal record, access to an assault rifle with enough ammunition and power to wipe out a neighborhood, as well as other weapons of violence that were registered to her. He committed matricide before his massacre of 20 children and 6 adults, followed by suicide. What was she thinking about? What ever happened to constructive parenting? There is nothing wrong with responsible gun ownership and teaching young adults about that responsibility, but a mental evaluation of the person behind the trigger has to be considered. There are many more instances of schoolchildren bringing guns to school and ultimately killing teachers, students and committing suicide. One recent incident in particular was in Nevada where a 12-year old shot and killed a math teacher/coach and shot two other children as well as committed suicide. Police stated that he "brought the gun from home". Another case was the 14-year old (Phillip Chism) who was asked by his teacher to stay after school, before he cut her throat in an upstairs bathroom and dumped her body in a nearby woods area. Where did he learn this murderous behavior? Why did he choose his teacher to be an enemy?

With respect to recent shooting violence since the verdict, Renisha McBride, 19, was shot to death in her quest for help, by knocking on a local neighbor's door following a car accident in Detroit. It seems apparent that the homeowner had a choice whether or not to open his door. In choosing to open the door he immediately shot McBride in the head, originally claiming that the gun went off by accident. Amid the excitement of growing protest, the killer was not originally arrested or charged, claiming the self-defense "stand your ground" law, when he, in fact, was defending himself by having the door closed (locked) in the first place. In another case, a black ex-college football player, Jonathan Ferrell, was also shot to death by a policeman while approaching him in need of help, similar to Renisha McBride. Ferrell was obviously distraught following a car accident and was perceived by the officer as "threatening". Other cops on the scene did not perceive a threat and did not fire a shot. Various non-lethal methods of stopping potential aggression that the officer had at his disposal could have been applied, but he chose to use deadly force. Another case involves a white man, Michael Dunn, who opened fire into a car at the three black teenagers of whom he felt were "playing their music too loud" at a gas station in Jacksonville, Florida. One of the teens, the driver of the vehicle, Jordan Davis, 17, was killed. Each of these incidents happened subsequent to the watchman verdict. Two of these cases are being defended as "stand your ground" and all of these incidents are perceived as racial. Did the watchman verdict set a new precedent as to the legal discharge of a firearm, while confusing others? Do others want to copy the watchman in hopes of getting rich? There have been many subsequent homicides of black youth since the verdict. And in the same manner, the shooter gets in the media, sets up a GoFundMe account and becomes wealthy almost overnight; *applauded and paid for the act of killing a black person from the beginning, regardless of guilt.* Was the watchman verdict the grey clouds that portend a storm? Is there a coincidence that all three of these victims are black? With respect to the recent shooting massacre at the Washington Navy Yard that killed 12 innocent people, the shooter possessed an identical AR-15 assault rifle to the one that was used in the Connecticut schoolchildren massacre of less than a year before. Why do these mass murders continue to re-occur? Why and for what purpose are *war weapons* being made available to the general public? According to reader William Taylor, who wrote to the New York Daily News (9/21/13 p. 21), "The Constitution provides the right to bear arms but does not define what qualifies as arms therefore, why am I not able to own a fighter jet or a nuclear weapon? Because common sense says so! The same common sense should not allow me the right to possess a weapon with the capability of killing dozens of people in a few seconds". Also, why is the video game industry allowed to produce virtual reality/ simulated games of violence, including directions of how to take apart, put together, load, unload and operate actual weapons of violence and death; as well as simulated games of robbery, burglary, car-jacking/ assault, terrorism, war, among others, and direct them to such impressionable groups as kids and teenagers. Are we also creating the criminal element in our society? What ever happened to Pac Man and Super Mario? Another reader, J. Crestwell Munnings wrote to the Daily News (9/21/13), "There is an epidemic of gun violence in our nation. Guns are like pizzas to young and impressionable minds. Too many of our children are exposed to guns and malicious video games that fascinate/ glorify violence and killing". Who can dispute that guns and violence are part of our culture, not to mention the recent terrorist attacks on American soil. Parents have a responsibility not to feed into this madness. Why are we training our children to be violent? What message are we sending them?

Throughout history, it has always been the great adult leaders who were assassinated in behalf of the country's problems, and now it's the children who are being executed because of the adult inability to find a solution to those continuing problems. The children are our new martyrs. Why is Congress allowing this? In the same paragraph (NY Daily News 9/21 p. 21) William Taylor states, "Some people treat our founding fathers as infallible and their writings as Holy Scripture. They created a document that Ben Franklin claimed as 'not perfect, but the best that could be done under the circumstances'. Had these men been able to foresee the efficiency we have developed in killing each other, they may have had second thoughts about the Second Amendment". Why has Congress been so uncooperative with Obama throughout his presidency? He wanted to save lives. These people are adults and they are killing our children, either directly or indirectly, and these are all of our kids. We're supposed to guide and protect them, not expose them to danger or hurt them. The children at Sandy Hook Elementary were innocent, Emmett Till did nothing wrong and the teenaged suspect was not a suspicious character or a "thug". They were our children, no different than yours.

In summation, the social significance of this homicide together with "stand your ground" legislation is that this law acts as a license to kill. The deceased teenager never had to lay a hand on the watchman to kill him, claim self-defense, and win the ensuing case. All that the watchman had to do was provoke him into an altercation, preferably in a shaded area, kill him, and receive a not guilty verdict. Dead men can't testify. He could have had a previous vendetta against the teenager and knew he would execute him. Was he so confident that he would be found not guilty that he carried out his intended plan? Did he perceive black life as so insignificant that it helped to boost his confidence during this action? Even if this case wasn't about race or self-defense, it was something that did not have to happen and could have been avoided; and that's what makes it a crime. The watchman could have chosen countless other options or avoided the situation entirely, but he did what he wanted to do.

The final verdict of this case is significant by the number of areas it presents (i.e. race, gun control, child safety, etc.), but it leaves society in a dilemma over the questions of morality and equality, once again in American history. The incident and verdict have grown into larger issues concerning the safety of children. The aim is to prevent further child gunshot victims, especially at the hands of adults.

Social reforms should also be created for the removal of inequality of all phases of life/society and the racial profiling of unsuspecting victims. Developments concerning the area of racial profiling reveal new instances of discrimination. In NYC, three black people were stopped, arrested and detained for allegedly using fake credit/ debit cards after the completion of their purchases and after having left the stores, most notably the world-renowned Barney's and Macy's Department stores. All three were false arrests and one included a noted actor. When will the discrimination end? Have blacks ever lived on an equal plane to whites in America? After the assassination of Abraham Lincoln, President Andrew Johnson said, "I am against freeing slaves. This is a country for white men. As long as I'm President, this will be a government of white men." Most negative international critique against America has to do with historic race relations. They have trouble in their rationalization and view of America as the land of freedom, equality and opportunity, as many view America as the face of corruption. America has only itself to blame for this negative view. Millions of people around the world did not accept this verdict, as well as other atrocious verdicts stemming from racial incidents in modern American history. Society may deteriorate even further than it has if this verdict isn't rectified. The verdict has led the country into the state that it is in now, a state of disarray. All of the energy and support for the watchman has somehow been harnessed into a political party, and has elected a President.

The watchman verdict is no different than the verdict that freed the murderers of Emmett Till in 1955, and the murderers who killed the four little girls in an Alabama Sunday School in 1963, among other atrocious racially-induced verdicts in American history. The proper name for this type of justice should properly be called, "injustice". Why would a man with a loaded gun in pursuit of an unarmed teenager need to cry for help? Who was the more likely party that would have cried for help in that situation? To say that it was the watchman's voice, then you are simultaneously silencing the victim's testimony; and you are also part of the problem. In effect, the jury convicted the deceased for his own murder, and not by a jury of his peers; a dead child without a voice. According to the defense, the watchman delivered his testimony before his day in court; and it appears that the teenager did not utter a single word during the trial.

CPSIA information can be obtained
at www.ICGtesting.com
Printed in the USA
LVHW112107090919
630430LV00002B/374/P